# SPECIFIC LEARNING DIFFICULTIES IN MATHEMATICS: A CLASSROOM APPROACH

NAGGAR

## A NASEN Publication

Published in 1996
Reprinted in 2001

ISBN 0 906730 81 3

Published by NASEN.
NASEN is a registered charity. Charity No. 1007023.
NASEN is a company limited by guarantee, registered in England and Wales.
Company No. 2674379.

Further copies of this book and details of NASEN's many other publications may be obtained from the Publications Department at its registered office:
NASEN House, 4/5 Amber Business Village, Amber Close, Amington, Tamworth, Staffs. B77 4RP.
Tel: 01827 311500; Fax: 01827 313005; Email: welcome@nasen.org.uk
Website: www.nasen.org.uk

Copy editing by Nicola von Schreiber.
Cover design by Graphic Images.
Typeset in Times by J. C. Typesetting and printed in the United Kingdom by Stowes.

# SPECIFIC LEARNING DIFFICULTIES IN MATHEMATICS: A CLASSROOM APPROACH

## Contents

# SPECIFIC LEARNING DIFFICULTIES IN MATHEMATICS: A CLASSROOM APPROACH

## Introduction

The NASEN Mathematics Working Party, a section of the Association's Curriculum Subcommittee, was established to promote and support mathematical education in the interest of pupils with special educational needs. This publication represents the experience and views of members of the Working Party, in particular Lila Bental, Olwen El-Naggar, Margaret Stephens and Alec Williams. It has been collated and compiled by Olwen El-Naggar.

The NASEN Specific Learning Difficulties (SpLD) in Mathematics Initiative arose from requests from classroom teachers for practical guidance on providing classroom-based provision for pupils with SpLD in mathematics, which also offers the breadth and balance of opportunity required by the National Curriculum. This publication is thus intended to assist teachers to meet these needs and, because the guidance which is offered is general, it may also be useful to teachers with specialist responsibilities for pupils with SpLd.

In mathematics there is no 'received wisdom' regarding SpLD as may be claimed in the teaching of language skills. We are at the stage of assessing and evaluating the outcomes of teaching by experienced teachers. Teachers generally are recognising unusual and baffling responses in mathematics and may perhaps be associating these with 'dyslexia'. It is the view of the Working Party that the use of any umbrella term such as 'dyslexia' or 'dyscalculia' in the identification of educational needs should be viewed with caution, as there is a danger that generalisations arising could disregard the individual behaviour and responses of pupils covered by the term. It seems sensible not to assume that a pupil is suffering from 'dyslexia' or 'dyscalculia' but rather to investigate a wide range of possibilities, some of which could be teacher-generated. We see the difficulties as being specific to the individual learner, hence the justification for the term Specific Learning Difficulties (SpLD) which is used throughout this publication.

There is a frequent assumption that the approach to teaching pupils with SpLD should be wholly or predominantly on a one-to-one basis. Whatever the validity of that assumption, the fact remains that in practice, the majority of pupils with SpLD in mathematics must rely for their teaching on their own teacher working in normal classroom conditions. This publication is intended to inform and support the class teacher in the fulfilment of this responsibility with particular reference to the identification, assessment, prescriptive teaching and curricular needs of such pupils.

# Chapter 1 – Entitlement to Good Practice

Good practice takes many different forms. The exact approach that a school has decided to adopt will be identified in the school's mathematics policy document. When looking for references to good practice to include in such documents, schools frequently use the recommendations of the Cockcroft Report, *Mathematics Counts* (DES, 1982). In preparing guidance on what is good practice for pupils with SpLD it will also be necessary to draw on the recommendations of this document. What is good practice for all children is also likely to be good practice for pupils with SpLD.

The revised *Orders for the National Curriculum* (DfE, 1995) encourage a pupil-orientated approach to teaching and learning, allowing flexibility in selecting materials from earlier or later Key Stages and leaving schools to decide which items to cover in depth. This enables teachers to match the curriculum to the learning needs of all pupils within their schools.

The *Code of Practice on the Identification and Assessment of Special Educational Needs* (DfE, 1994) recommends a *staged* model of special educational needs in which the *first three* of its *five stages* are school-based. Although teachers may, as necessary, call upon the help of external specialists it is anticipated that the majority of the assessment and teaching in the early stages will be undertaken by the school. In most cases this will need to be through a differentiated approach, as appropriate within each progressive stage of the *Code of Practice*. It is, therefore, important that teachers make reference to school mathematics policy documents when preparing Individual Education Plans (IEPs) for pupils with specific learning difficulties in mathematics. A small number of these pupils will eventually hold statements advocating individual teaching from a specialist teacher for a few hours each week; many of them will not.

The essential element of discussion in mathematics (between the teacher and pupils as a group and between pupils themselves) is emphasised in both the Cockcroft Report, and the revised *National Curriculum Orders* (DfE, 1995). Such discussion cannot be provided through individual teaching programmes, as it is extremely difficult for us as adults to recapture intellectual naivety by imagining ourselves in a pre-understanding position. Children can often offer valid alternatives. Cockcroft emphasises the importance of classroom discussion for all pupils regardless of what stage they are at:

> While one aspect of mental mathematics is work 'in the head', another is the promotion of mathematical discussion in the classroom... There are some skills, puzzles and problems which are appropriate for every child no matter what stage of learning he may have reached and short class sessions can be arranged for work of this kind... (*Mathematics Counts*, para. 317)

### The mathematics/language relationship

It is through discussion and debate that logic and reasoning develop. Opportunities for *group* discussion, sensitively led by the perceptive class teacher, is an advantage denied to the child in one-to-one teaching. Mathematics reasoning and logic are dependent upon mathematics language and the concepts of its vocabulary can only be understood in context. Both the revised *National Curriculum Orders* and the document *Planning the Curriculum at Key Stages 1 and 2* (SCAA, 1995) encourage schools to plan a curriculum that offers equal access to all pupils through increased differentiation. Therefore, the necessity of *individualising* as distinct from *individual* teaching must be stressed (see page 30).

The correlation between poor reading and poor mathematics skills is addressed by Miles and Miles in their book, *Dyslexia and Mathematics* (1992). We welcome this book and find it generally helpful. The authors do, however, emphasise that this is a book predominantly about 'dyslexia' and make no claim to its being about good practice in teaching mathematics in general.

> ... We should like to make it clear that this is a book about dyslexia (or, strictly, specific developmental dyslexia), not about 'good practice' in teaching mathematics in general. (*Dyslexia and Mathematics*, page xii Preface)

There are dangers in assuming that the principles underlying general good practice are necessarily different from those applicable to teaching SpLD pupils. If there are strong links between SpLD in language and SpLD in mathematics, then collaborative planning between language support teachers and mathematics teachers is essential. At the moment examples of any such planning are rare.

Many teachers who are language support specialists are now being required to teach mathematics, with little or no training for their new role. Rarely, if ever, do we find the same degree of seriousness applied to teaching of mathematics to SpLD pupils as we do to the teaching of language skills. Many accepted works on mathematics and SpLD draw almost exclusively on experience from SpLD language teachers. The Cockcroft Committee expresses concern that pupils with learning difficulties in mathematics are often being taught by teachers who:

> ... concentrate largely on language work and are not always skilled in the teaching of mathematics or in the diagnosis of associated learning difficulties... (*Mathematics Counts*, para. 337)

Many well-intentioned teachers remove all written language from programmes for pupils with SpLD in the belief that this will give their pupils time to concentrate on the mathematics involved. This is, presumably, because SpLD pupils experience great difficulty with language in one or more areas of the English curriculum. The Cockcroft Report emphasises the importance of supporting pupils in their understanding of mathematics language:

> ... The policy of trying to avoid reading difficulties by preparing work cards in which the use of language is minimised or avoided altogether should not be adopted. Instead the necessary language skills should be developed through discussion and explanation and by encouraging children to talk and write about the investigations which they have undertaken... (*Mathematics Counts*, para. 311)

Although the revised National Curriculum Orders emphasise the language of mathematics, we seldom see language written into mathematics programmes. SpLD pupils can be assisted to access this important area of mathematics by the use of word processors, spell-checkers, concept keyboards and tape recorders. Language support in mathematics should be closely linked to that given in other areas of the curriculum (see pages 27 – 28).

### Curricular breadth, balance and relevance for pupils with SpLD in mathematics

When writing IEPs in mathematics the urgency of having to prepare documentation often prevents teachers from looking for breadth and balance of opportunity. There is always the danger of such programmes being reduced to the technique of pinpointing specific difficulties at the final symbolic stage (when the difficulty is not to do with writing numerals) and suggesting instrumental remediation (ie rules without reasons).

eg
$$51$$
$$- 12$$

In trying to read the above sum a child said, 'Five take away one makes four and two take away one makes one.'

Instrumental remediation

The teacher's explanation of how to do the sum was:

'Two from one you can't, so cross out the five and put a four. You put the one with the other one to give eleven. Now two from eleven leaves nine and one from four leaves three.'

$$51$$
$$- 12$$
$$39$$

The Cockcroft Report recommends that we present our pupils with a collection of like experiences from which *they* can extract the concept. This is often misunderstood, resulting in programmes that concentrate entirely on the practice of skills. The learners are then subjected to a battery of examples and explanation. When they can master the task at hand, for example subtraction sums, it is declared that they can now subtract, but can they?

- Do they know when and where to use it?

- Do they know that when they give change they usually 'add on'?

- Can they see when to round up or down before subtracting to make the task easier?

- Can they estimate what the answer is likely to be?

- Can they think of something else to do if they cannot remember the technique?

- Finally, do they know that they can use a calculator, and how and when to use it?

Richard Skemp's 'relational' and 'instrumental' concepts detailed in *The Psychology of Learning Mathematics* (1971) and elaborated on by Chinn in *Dyslexia and Mathematics* (1992) are central to the problems in this field. Pupils often can master specific skills on an instrumental basis but tend to be unable to transfer, estimate, approximate or give any other indication of understanding the relationship involved. Formulation of their own mathematics from (perhaps, quite simple) reality situations is not very often tried or considered.

In order to keep focus on balance, breadth and relevance while at the same time assisting pupils to cope with their specific difficulties, the advice outlined in para. 243 of the Cockcroft

Report, '... We believe that there are certain elements which need to be present in successful mathematics teaching to pupils of all ages', should be considered:

- exposition by the teacher;

- discussion between teacher and pupils and between pupils themselves;

- appropriate practical work;

- consolidation and practice of fundamental skills and routines;

- problem solving, including the application of mathematics to everyday situations;

- investigational work.

If we couple together investigations and problem solving (and are not sidetracked by trying to define them individually), then the following programme is applicable:

Step 1: A clear explanation of what we expect our pupils to do, inviting questions and discussion.

Step 2: Provision of materials and time for them to understand that explanation in their own way, while working together and discussing (through games, puzzles, problems and role playing).

Step 3: Recording and reinforcing through the use of work cards, text books and recording individual/group activity results.

Pupils with SpLD could experience difficulties with any or all of the suggested steps in this model (see Chapter 3). By encouraging every pupil to develop his or her own strategies for overcoming difficulties, and to respect and value all valid solutions offered by their peers, teachers can alleviate some of the anxieties felt by pupils with SpLD. The frustration of not being able to conform is a major factor in demotivation. More efficient methods can be demonstrated but individual strategies should be respected by both teacher and pupils. Implementation of such a model would be largely negated if exclusively one-to-one teaching were employed.

**Conclusion**

The National Curriculum tells us what to teach. How to teach it is left to individual classroom teachers. Headteachers and their staff set policies on identification and provision for pupils with special needs and the teaching of mathematics. Class teachers set the pace and style for learning within the framework of these policies and their resulting schemes of work within their own classrooms. It is the responsibility of those teaching pupils with SpLD to assist them, to the greatest possible extent, to access the full curriculum by making the strategies of both teacher and learner efficient and effective.

The emphasis of both the Cockcroft Report and the National Curriculum, that good practice is a right for all pupils, should be observed in all writings on this subject. It is only by giving equal emphasis to the quality of teaching in both language and mathematics that we can provide pupils with SpLD with equality of opportunity to learn.

# Chapter 2 – Gathering Information

**Assessment**

The staged approached to the identification of special needs required by the *Code of Practice* determines that prior to referral for pupil evaluation, the pupil's learning problem shall be addressed at the school level. In the vast majority of cases, documented evidence which indicates that general educational alternatives have been attempted and evaluated will need to be submitted with any applications for statementing. Learning difficulties in mathematics, whether linked with SpLD or not, will vary with individuals. It is, therefore, important to assess each pupil's strengths and weaknesses and plan accordingly.

Schools are required to gather information on individual students from a variety of sources, including the pupil, parent or carer, and teachers. Early medical checks are also advisable to make sure that there are no hearing or visual defects. The information gained from these sources will need to be collated and examined together, with a view to creating a teaching/learning programme.

The following pages make some suggestions about the type of assessment that could prove useful when planning IEPs in mathematics for pupils with SpLD.

A leaflet, *'Specific Learning Difficulties in Mathematics'* published by the British Dyslexia Association, states that: '...failure in one scholastic area is often linked to failure in others ...' The same document also suggests that as written language and mathematics are symbolic, they will be processed in the same area of the brain and, hence, will both require: ordering and sequencing; short-term memory; labelling; learning; and remembering. When available, information from previous assessment in any of these areas is likely to be of significance in understanding learning difficulties in mathematics of pupils with SpLD. Classroom implications for identification and remediation in these areas follows in Chapter 3.

**What do we need from assessment?**

The following information is important when planning mathematics programmes for all children, but particularly so for those with a specific difficulty. Where possible, assessment criteria have been grouped under National Curriculum Attainment Targets (ATs).

*The pupil's level of ability in using and applying mathematics*
(National Curriculum AT 1: Using and Applying Mathematics)

Only teachers give anyone ready-made sums. In real life, individuals must formulate their own mathematics. For this they need to be able to abstract the data from the situation, select the appropriate process(es), estimate or approximate an answer, and carry it out, and to place and assess the answer in the context of the original situation.

These processes can present problems to any child, particularly if previous mathematics experience has been dominated by context-free, ready-formulated sums. For the pupil with SpLD, opportunities to formulate mathematics from everyday happenings and situations must form a substantial, systematised part of the mathematics curriculum. If few such challenges have been experienced, assessment in this area is likely to be non-productive.

*The pupil's use of mathematical language*
(National Curriculum AT 1: Using and Applying Mathematics)

For many pupils with SpLD, the discrepancy between mathematical terms and the reality it represents can be both wide and confusing. Knowledge of a word, both receptively and expressively, is no guarantee of understanding. Accurate classroom assessment of spoken language, particularly expressive, poses particular problems. Practical situations and the use of apparatus is likely to be essential, notably in assessing a spatial vocabulary including terms such as under, through, opposite and between.

### The pupil's ability to see links
(National Curriculum AT 1: Using and Applying Mathematics)

In mathematics, the purpose of assessment in this area is twofold: firstly to provide information about the pupil's ability to link the concept level and the symbolic level of understanding; secondly to assess the pupil's ability to see links between various aspects of mathematics. Examples include fractions and decimal numbers, the commutative law in addition (3 + 4 is another way of saying 4 + 3) and the commutative law of multiplication (3 x 4 is another way of saying 4 x 3). These concepts need to be internalised and are, therefore, heavily dependent on long-term memory. If the concept is already understood, pupils will merely have to decode the symbols concerned.

### The pupil's level of understanding of the number system
(National Curriculum AT 2: Number)

Assessment in this most fundamental area must, in the first place, seek to determine what the pupil *is* able to do and understand. From aspects of mathematics which are sequential in nature, assessment must then seek to identify those procedures, concepts and skills at which the breakdown is occurring. Such instances are to be regarded not as errors, but as *'miscues'*, giving valuable information as to the nature of the thinking involved. This particularly applies to all stages in the introduction and use of place value. Conclusions should not be attempted on the basis of a single miscue. Presenting further analogous examples provides the opportunity to determine whether or not it represents an established pattern of approach.

### The pupil's use of mathematical symbols
(National Curriculum AT 2: Number)

Difficulties can obviously arise in any situation where a mathematical problem is presented to the pupil wholly or partly in written form. The actual formation of mathematical signs and symbols and the order in which they are required to be presented may pose some difficulty. This will be evident in many aspects of place value.

Many pupils with SpLD will present an unconventional or idiosyncratic layout of mathematical operations, which can form a barrier to further progress and understanding. An example of this is column displacement in setting down algorithms. Therefore, assessment in the use of mathematical symbols may need to be carried out, not only by checking written examples but also by:

- listening to the pupil read symbols aloud;

- presenting a task in written symbols for the pupil to carry out (using apparatus);

- asking the pupil to write down in symbols a problem presented orally.

### The pupil's level of understanding of shape and space
(National Curriculum AT 3: Shape Space and Measures)

Deficiencies and inconsistencies in visual perception, perhaps related to confusion in laterality, can account for poor performance in spatial assessment. Even in the case of pupils with abilities in other areas, an activity such as 'posting' differing plastic shapes into corresponding holes in a container lid can present formidable problems. As in other areas, the assessment procedure must commence at elementary levels, preferably with the pupil being asked to verbalise on what is being attempted. Much assessment in the spatial area should be carried out with objects that can be handled in preference to pictures, diagrams and other similar representations.

### The pupil's level of understanding of measures
(National Curriculum AT 3: Shape Space and Measures)

Understanding and making use of measures presupposes a background of relevant practical experience, the acquisition of an appropriate vocabulary, making comparisons, estimating and approximating, and the ability to generalise. The inconsistencies in memorising and response characteristic of pupils with SpLD are such that the process of assessment in the use of any one measure must take account of these factors, particularly the ability to estimate and make comparisons.

### The pupil's use of compensatory strategies

Many pupils with SpLD find their own (sometimes ingenious) ways of coping with their difficulties. An assessment of the type and effectiveness of these strategies is likely to prove helpful to the planning of work for these pupils. Many coping strategies involve finger counting or the use of tallying which can only be assessed through observation, therefore assessment would need to be through a combination of observation and discussion (see pages 18 – 21).

This following example was taken from a test paper of a 12 year-old boy who displayed poor understanding of place value.

Question:
$$240$$
$$- 186$$

He interpreted this initially as 24 take away 186. Then he said, 'Take away 40… that's 46 left and a hundred.'

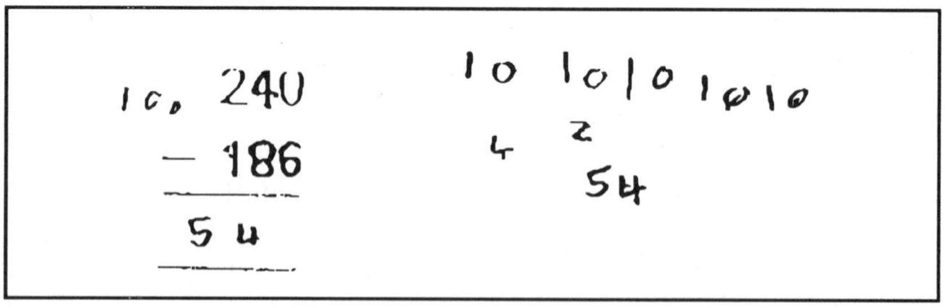

Figure 1.

He wrote the 100 on the left of the sum and, as he said '56, 66, 76, 86, 96', he wrote down five tens to the right of the sum (*Figure 1*). When he reached 96 he counted on to 100 with his fingers and said, 'that's four left over.' He added up the tens and wrote 54, the correct answer, under his calculations and then placed the answer under the sum but in the wrong columns. He was using his own strategy to solve the problem which involved complementary addition. What David had in fact done was:

$$240 = (200 + 40) \qquad 186 = (100 + 86)$$
$$(200 + 40) \quad - \quad (100 + 86)$$
$$= \quad 100 - 46$$
$$= \quad 54$$

His method, however, has limited applications.

### The pupil's concentration span

Concentration is governed by several factors, many of which are situational. Sometimes there are medical or sensory reasons for lack of concentration, in which case expert advice will be required. The problem could be a general one or it could be related only to mathematics. Observation during assessment can disclose both areas of interest and those of frustration. Assessment should be used to observe the pupil's preferred learning style, choice of apparatus and interests. Programmes can then be planned to provide interesting challenges.

### The pupil's accuracy of recording results

Difficulties with symbolic recordings have already been mentioned above (see page 11). A further aspect of inaccurate recording is when pupils present a totally unrealistic answer, perhaps because they have not asked themselves if it makes sense, but more often because they have misheard or misread the question. This could be through carelessness or because the explanation itself was unclear, but it could also be because the pupil has an auditory or visual perceptual difficulty. Asking the pupil to explain how he or she reached the answer is often the most useful form of assessment.

### The pupil's feelings about mathematics

Feelings about mathematics are not only influenced by the degree of both success and failure encountered over the years, but also by attitudes of parents (see page 17), peers and siblings. When teachers are planning mathematics programmes, they will need to know which areas promote positive feelings that will assist in learning, and which negative feelings that will hinder it.

Assessment of the pupil's feelings are gleaned from a variety of sources. Pupil interviews and parent/carer interviews (see pages 16–18) probably provide the best information, but previous knowledge (written records, information from teachers etc.) may provide significant information.

### Additional points

An in-depth analysis of the pupil's individual *error patterns* and *memory problems* is essential to the planning of programmes for pupils with SpLD. These will be highlighted through teacher observations.

Some very important points to be taken into consideration when assessing pupils' mathematics abilities should be:

a)  oral contribution (group or class);

b)  behaviour in group work, active or passive;

c)  asking for help, from whom, frequency;

d)  kind of help requested;

e)  use of apparatus/equipment;

f)  motivation, eagerness or procrastination;

g)  preferred learning style.

All the above additional factors can be gleaned from an informed observation of the pupil on a day-to-day basis rather than through specific assessment procedures. National Curriculum teacher assessment should provide useful information on many of these issues, particularly those that are directly linked to National Curriculum Programmes of Study.

**What type of assessment should we use?**

Effective assessment is likely to include a combination of:

- testing;

- pupil and parent/carer interviews;

- observation.

### Testing

It is the statutory right of all pupils to follow the National Curriculum. Assessment profiles should therefore include National Curriculum assessment, both teacher assessment and Standardised Assessment Tests or Tasks (SATs) when used. This assessment is essential to the planning of future provision through an inclusive programme of study. However, it will need to be supplemented so that a more detailed picture can be obtained.

### Do we need standardised tests?

The results of standardised tests have been analysed in relation to a large sample of children making it possible to say how a pupil compares with other pupils nationally. Such a test would give information on whether or not the pupil was in the lowest 20 per cent on a national scale. It would not however pinpoint individual strengths and weaknesses.

Tests which present a profile, such as NFER's *Profile of Mathematical Skills* (Norman France, 1979), can give some guidance under sectional headings but do not explain *why* a pupil has difficulties. The most effective approach is to ask the pupil to explain how he or she has worked out an example. Misreadings, misunderstandings, incorrect copying, partial knowledge and faulty procedures can emerge. What may also emerge are correct answers which have arisen from bizarre procedures (see page 12).

Tests which are designed to determine pupils' levels of attainment in particular skills or concepts are known as 'criterion referenced' tests, eg National Curriculum SATs and NFER's *Essential Mathematics Tests* (LM Bental, 1976). Results from these tests can assist teachers to make decisions regarding which children need help and the sort of help they need.

Support teachers frequently use published tests to identify baselines for differentiated lessons, but test material has limitations. For example in *Figure 2* and *Figure 3*.

In this example the teacher made a note of both the fact that John had difficulty counting backwards and that he was able to apply his own strategies to overcome his difficulties.

### Do we need a maths age?

A norm-related test such as the appropriate one from the NFER *Mathematics 7 – 11 Test Series* (Hagues and Courtenay, 1994) helps to establish whether the pupil is under-performing in comparison with others of the same age and gives a maths age. Items in such tests tend not to be 'weighted' according to type or level of difficulty. Thus, pupils with identical or near identical scores may have entirely differing abilities and weaknesses if an item analysis is made. Thus, a maths age derived from a composite score is neither relevant nor useful.

John (age 9 years 6 months)

Teacher observation while performing the following task from the *Basic Number Screening Test* (Gillham and Hesse).

This test is designed to give a quick assessment of a pupil's understanding of the basic principles underlying our number system (number concepts) and the processes involved in computation (number skills). The test makes no demands on reading ability since all instructions are given verbally.

In *Figure 2* John looked only at the columns that needed completing, ignoring the computation involved, and said of the units, '8, 7, 6 so the next one must be 5'. Looking at the tens column he said, 'Those are all ones so that must be a one as well'. In the solution column he followed the same logic and wrote in the eight units and then the two tens.

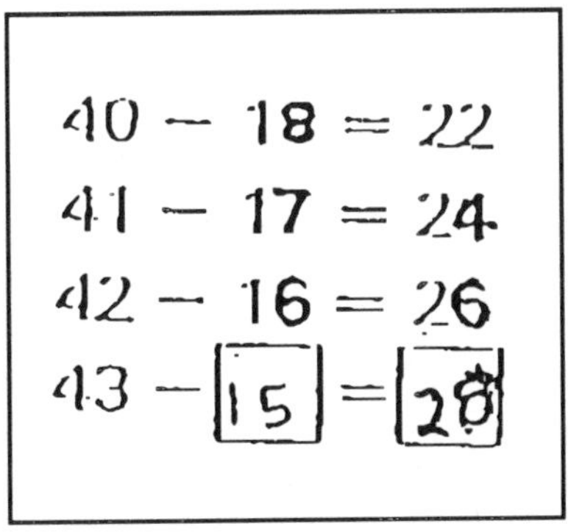

Figure 2.

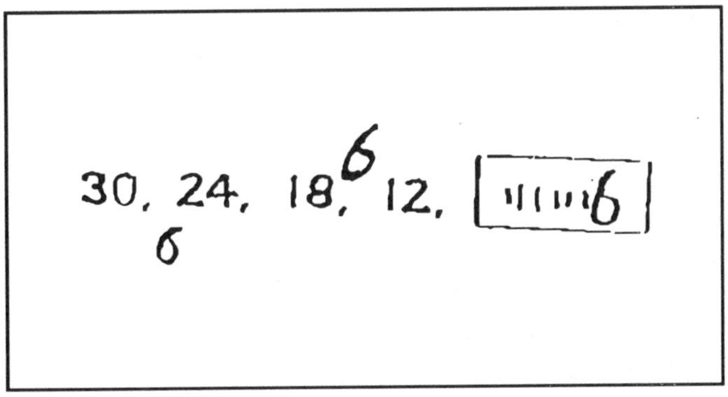

Figure 3.

In this example teacher-observation while the pupil was carrying out the test resulted in an understanding of his ability to look for pattern. However, an adherence to the test prevented the teacher from adding a further line to see what would happen when the rule no longer satisfied the answer. Valuable information is often lost by sticking too closely to commercially produced tests.

In *Figure 3* John noted that the numbers were getting smaller and proceeded to count backwards from 30 to 24. He found this very difficult even with the aid of his tally marks in the box. He then reversed the process and counted on from 18 to 24. He struggled to count backwards from 12 to 6 and was not confident that his answer was 6. The difficulty in counting backwards is one frequently encountered by pupils with specific learning difficulties.

*Pupil and parent/carer interviews*
*Pupil interviews*

The effectiveness of any assessment and intervention will be influenced by involvement and interest of the child or young person concerned. (*Code of Practice*, para. 234)

Aims:

- To identify as precisely as possible the aspects of mathematics with which the pupil is currently experiencing difficulty.

- To ascertain the likely causes of the difficulties and their links with the SpLD problem.

- To clarify the pupil's attitude to mathematics and to his or her learning problems.

- To identify the interests of the pupil which can be used to provide meaningful and acceptable contexts for the subsequent learning programme.

Most pupils are aware of their own individual strengths and weaknesses. Carefully planned interview questions can provide teachers with valuable information for programme planning, but when relevant sidetracking and follow-up questions should be included.

Questions that have proved useful when talking to pupils:

- Do you enjoy maths?

- Do you think you are good at maths? Why?

- Which bits do you think you are good at?

- What do you find most difficult? Why?

- Why do you think people learn maths?

- Do you think it is useful?

- Does anyone help you with your maths at home? If so, who?

- Have you got your own calculator?

- When do you use it?

- Do you enjoy using a computer?

- Do you have a computer at home?

These questions are by no means definitive but they do serve as a starting point for the busy classroom teacher. Where possible, responses should be taped and transcribed. Pupils could be encouraged to record their own answers. An example record sheet can be found on page 22. However, the use of a schedule should not preclude the use of supplementary questions which may provide information at greater depth.

*Examples of pupil responses to interviews*

Emma age 11

When asked why she disliked maths Emma disclosed that 'she knew nothing' and that the majority of maths was done from a textbook and she had great difficulty with lessons that were 'read and do'.


John age 9 years 6 months
Disclosed that he disliked maths which he finds most difficult. His comments included:

'It's complicated, very confusing and awkward.'
'You know times tables – they are very hard and I don't know what the line with the two dots on means.'
'If I knew how to read I'd find it easier. I'm sure I could do it then.'
'I have all the ideas in my head but I can't write them down.'


Michael age 14

'I know about nominators and denominators, but I don't know which goes where, and I'm not sure how to add them.'

*Parent/carer interviews*

… Children's progress will be diminished if their parents are not seen as partners in the educational process with unique knowledge and information to impart… (*Code of Practice* para. 2.28)

Aims:

- To obtain a balanced history of the pupil's learning development in terms of what seemed easy, what difficult; also the pupil's interests.

- To find out what mathematical experiences the pupil has had and is having outside school.

- To discover what the parent or carer is willing to do to support their child's mathematical learning.

- To clarify what the parent or carer sees as the pupil's learning priorities in mathematics. These may be general, eg to pass exams, or specific, eg to learn tables.

Questions that have proved useful when talking to parents/carers:

- Do you think _____ has a problem with maths?

- What does he/she find difficult?

- What are your main concerns about _____'s maths?

- Does anyone else in the family have difficulty with maths?

- What do you think the school can do about it?

- What would you be willing to do to help?
  (This would need to be followed with possible suggestions depending on both the child's present state of learning and the realms of possible provision within your school.)

An example record sheet can be found on page 23.

---

*Examples of responses to parent/carer interviews*

Parents and carers of pupils with SpLD tend to hold a variety of points of view on their child's mathematics learning, of which the following four are most frequently given:

1.  Their personal experience of mathematics was that it was a difficult subject to learn, they had negative feelings towards the subject and therefore they had low expectations of their child's mathematical understanding.

2.  They found mathematics difficult and therefore really wanted their child to 'do well'.

3.  They did not experience any difficulty with mathematics themselves and therefore could not understand the difficulties their child was experiencing.

4.  They perceived current mathematics as different to that which they were taught at school and therefore offered little or no help to their children.

---

***Observation***

By watching the pupil as he or she is working and discussing their work, teachers can discover whether skills such as counting, measurement or the use of drawing instruments are being used. It provides opportunity for pupils to clear up misunderstanding and correct their errors.

Diagnostic marking of written work, indicating where the mistake has occurred, together with either supportive comments or suggestions that the pupil should consult the teacher, provide vital information to be used for future programme planning. Intervention of this sort will need to be immediate if it is to be fully effective.

Aims of observation:

- To discover individual strategies.

- To reveal any unusual working patterns.

- To offer pupils the opportunity to reconsider what they have written or displayed.

- To check if basic skills have been mastered.

*Examples of observation*

Example 1: Gary age 10
Observing Gary during a group assessment activity revealed the fact that visual perceptual difficulties identified during his assessment for specific learning difficulties in language were apparent in mathematics.

Task:    Pupils were asked to record as many ways of making 20 as they could think of:

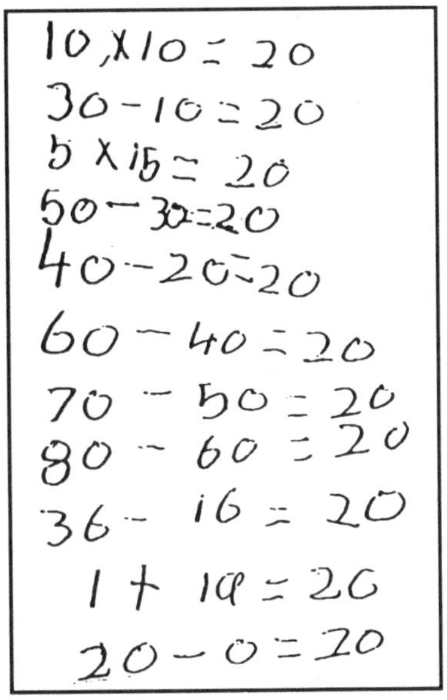

$$10 \times 10 = 20$$
$$30 - 10 = 20$$
$$5 \times 15 = 20$$
$$50 - 30 = 20$$
$$40 - 20 = 20$$
$$60 - 40 = 20$$
$$70 - 50 = 20$$
$$80 - 60 = 20$$
$$36 - 16 = 20$$
$$1 + 19 = 20$$
$$20 - 0 = 20$$

*Figure 4.*

Most of Gary's examples (*Figure 4*) were subtraction from complete tens with no units. There are no examples of division. The single example of addition is correct but the examples written with the multiplication sign have been added. Gary has visual discrimination problems with letters, particularly b and d, both in reading and writing.

The teacher wrote two examples (*Figure 5*) for him to complete, in order to check that his own examples were not due to careless writing on his part. His solution confirmed the difficulty he has discriminating between similar shapes in different orientation. When the teacher discussed this matter with him he said, 'I know the difference but the signs seem to get jumbled up in my head.'

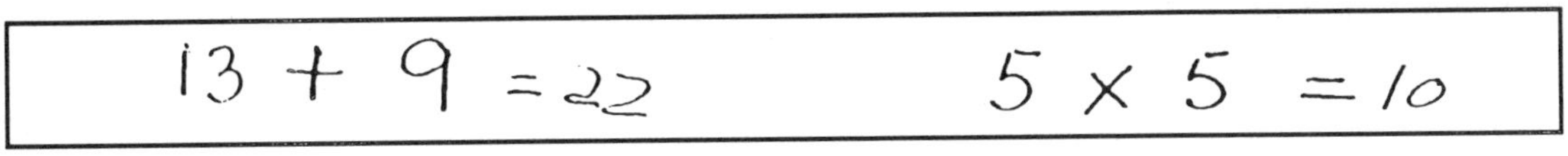

$$13 + 9 = 22 \qquad 5 \times 5 = 10$$

*Figure 5.*

The teacher then drew a multiplication sign on a square of paper using the diagonals of the square (*Figure 6*).

*Figure 6.*

Gary was then asked to give examples of making 20 using both this sign and a division sign. He did this successfully displaying an understanding of the processes involved.

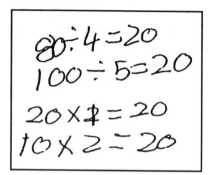

*Figure 7.*

Squares of card with +, -, ÷, x signs on them were included in his programme.

---

Example 2: Ian age 12

Ian, who understands addition at the concrete stage, has no difficulty recording the results of practical addition and subtraction to ten. However, when presented with abstract situations in the form of symbolic subtraction 'sums', the answers were always the first number in the equation.

eg 6 - 3 = 6

When asked to explain his working Ian verbalised, 'six take away the three (covering up the three with his hand) … there's the six left.' When the connection to the concrete examples was pointed out to him he was really surprised. 'Oh, so that's what it means!' No problems from then on.

---

Example 3: Sally age 10 years 6 months

Sally was working horizontal additions and producing some very strange answers without discernable patterns.

eg 5 + 4 = 8

When asked to explain how she arrived at her answer Sally verbalised, 'Five add four … you take the five and then you say six (pencil traced the down stroke of the numeral four), seven (pencil traced the horizontal stroke of the four), eight (pencil traced the horizontal stroke of the four), so the answer is eight.'

Sally was confusing the numeral four with tally marks. What was really alarming was the length of time that the errors in Examples 2 and 3 had gone undetected.

Example 4: Emma age 12

Emma finds place value difficult, at least she does when she has to record it.

|        |                                                                    |
|--------|--------------------------------------------------------------------|
| 68     | Emma used the algorithm she had been taught. She worked aloud 8 - 5 |
| - 5    | and 6 - 5. When asked to estimate the answer she said she thought it |
| ——     | would be about 60.                                                 |

Emma worked several further problems in the same way. She understood the concept but had difficulty positioning the numbers.

## Conclusion

Through observation and intervention during assessment, teachers are able to probe further into the reasons for incorrect results. In the above examples (all of which *appeared* to indicate SpLD) Examples 1 and 4 both indicated specific learning difficulties. Examples 2 and 3, which could without observation and intervention during assessment have been interpreted as SpLD, in fact turned out to be errors caused by misunderstanding.

**Sample record sheets**
Specific Learning Difficulties in Mathematics: A Classroom Approach

| PUPIL INTERVIEWS | | |
|---|---|---|
| NAME: | DATE OF BIRTH: | CLASS: |

a) Do you enjoy maths?

b) Do you think you are good at maths? Why?

c) Which bits do you think you are good at?

d) What do you find most difficult? Why?

e) Why do you think people learn maths?

f) What would you like to learn in maths?

g) Does anyone help you with your maths at home? If so, who?

h) Have you got your own calculator?
   When do you use it?

i) Do you enjoy using a computer?
   Do you have a computer at home?

| PARENT/CARER INTERVIEWS | | |
|---|---|---|
| NAME: | DATE OF BIRTH: | CLASS: |

a) Do you think _____ has a problem with maths?

b) What does he/she find difficult? Why?

c) What are your main concerns about _____ ?

d) Does anyone else in the family have difficulty with maths?

e) What do you think the school can do to help?

f) What would you be willing to do to help?

# Chapter 3 – Identifying Specific Learning Difficulties in Mathematics

Many people have difficulties learning mathematics; they may or may not have SpLD. The purpose of the following is not to label or categorise the pupil, but to develop as total a picture as possible of both the assets and shortcomings that he or she brings to mathematics learning. Difficulties in the designated areas should not be conceived as being exclusive to pupils with SpLD. However, when the total picture obtained suggests the likelihood of the existence of specific learning difficulties, a combination of the characteristics may be apparent.

## Check-list of characteristics

1. *Short-term memory/working memory*
   Pupils may experience difficulty with:
   - remembering the sequence of instructions;
   - problem solving;
   - limited memory storage, causing overload and total loss of focus on the task in hand.

2. *Long-term memory difficulties*
   Pupils may experience difficulty with:
   - remembering routines;
   - linking different mathematics topics;
   - remembering algorithms;
   - recalling tables.

3. *Directional confusion*
   Pupils may experience difficulty with:
   - consistently starting computation from the correct place;
   - consistently writing numbers the correct way around;
   - remembering right and left;
   - working around the decimal point;
   - working on number lines;
   - rotation.

4. *Visual perceptual difficulties*
   Pupils may experience difficulty with:
   - the identification of similar signs and numerals, eg + and x, 5 and 3, 6 and 9, ÷ and -, < >;
   - identifying similar geometric shapes, eg different types of triangle.

5. *Sequencing problems*
   Pupils may experience difficulty with:
   - counting backwards;
   - counting forwards across the decades and the hundreds;
   - sequencing days of the week, months of the year;
   - appreciation of sequential pattern;
   - recalling tables;
   - ordering tasks.

6. *Spatial awareness*
Pupils may experience difficulty with:
- place value;
- copying from the board, book or workcard;
- identifying spacial patterns;
- nominators and denominators;
- representing three-dimensional figures in two dimensions, and recognising the two-dimensional drawing corresponding to a given solid.

7. *Mathematics language*
Pupils may experience difficulty with:
- working with verbal 'sums';
- reading and understanding mathematical questions;
- consistently naming signs and symbols;
- double-meaning words, eg unit (could be kitchen unit).

8. *Lack of problem solving strategies*
Pupils may experience difficulty with:
- knowing what to do and why;
- thinking logically;
- linking reality to symbols and symbols to reality;
- drawing helpful diagrams.

9. *Motor perception difficulties*
Pupils may experience difficulty with:
- appropriate handling of measuring instruments;
- drawing diagrams;
- copying shapes.

If several of the items in the check-list of characteristics do appear consistently in a pupil's profile, they are likely to affect more than one aspect of mathematics learning. The following examples highlight some of the areas that could be affected and offer teachers guidance on ways in which they may help their pupils surmount their difficulties.

## Memory difficulties

Data held in the short-term memory is only held for a moment or two. Often several instructions need to be held at the same time (particularly for problem solving activities). For some items, such as recall of basic number facts, the wider the experience at the initial stage the more likely pupils are to transfer the information to long-term memory, where it can be stored and retrieved at a later date. Short-term memory difficulties result in pupils being unable to follow more than one instruction at a time. This means they are constantly falling behind their classmates, who may be confidently carrying out a three-stage task. The SpLD pupil may be seen by the teacher as disruptive because she or he keeps asking classmates for help.
*Teachers may help by:*

- Sitting the pupil near the teacher so that reminders can be given more easily.

- Checking written work frequently so that errors can be dealt with while the pupil still remembers what the task was.

- Making sure that homework tasks are clearly set out in detail so that instructions will not be forgotten.

- Making memory aids, such as written tables and charts, diagrams and calculators, available alongside other classroom apparatus.

- Making sure pupils can use calculators.

- Simple 'recipes' (reminders of order of working) with examples could be kept in a small reference notebook or written as 'post-its' (gummed labels or an envelope to hold notes) and stuck in the front of the book.

- Assisting pupils to develop mnemonics (taking the initial letters of a sequence of facts or a single word and using them to make a sentence).

- Teaching rhymes, eg 'Thirty days hath September', as memory props.

- Building 'rehearsal' of familiar facts into the programme.

### Sequencing and directional difficulties

Faulty sequencing affects recognition of number patterns. One important manifestation of this difficulty is in the recording of place value. The confusion with reading and recording numbers from left to right and working computation sums from right to left is a major problem. This is not helped by the fact that pupils' thinking does not always match techniques taught in the classroom, eg when adding sums of money it is common to add the pounds first and then the pence, whereas written computation of money starts with the pence.

*Teachers may help by:*

- Making calculators available at all times.

- Providing squared paper with an indicator to mark left and providing guidance on setting out 'sums' on squared paper.

- Providing practice in using small numbers (where results are easy to estimate) to help pupils to check their own procedures.

- Estimating using large numbers could be tackled by teaching pupils to 'round up' or down to the nearest ten before making a rough estimate.

- Placing the hundreds, tens and units (HTU) headings on each computation 'sum'.

- Discussing differences between mental and paper and pencil calculations.

- Making sure that calculations carried out mentally or with the aid of apparatus are accurately recorded.

### Visual perceptual difficulties

Problems with visual perception manifest themselves in many different ways across all mathematics topics. Those creating the greatest difficulties are those concerning symbolic recording, ie numerals and function signs.

*Teachers may help by:*

- Teaching the writing of numerals in groups where numerals (3 and 5) and (6 and 9) do not occur in the same groups, ie 1, 2, 3 making sure that 3 is correctly formed before introducing 4, 5, 6, and making sure that 6 is correctly formed before introducing 7, 8, 9, 10.

- Providing pupils with stencils.

- Placing the x and + signs on different coloured card squares, with the x sign forming the diagonals of the square; referring to the + sign as north and south signs; placing the ÷ and - signs on different coloured card squares and exaggerating the dots on the ÷ sign.

- Relating < and > to movement on a number line.

## Reading difficulties

Mathematical thinking is expressed in a precise language, using words, sentences, signs and symbols. New concepts represented by single words must ultimately be set in a language context for an improvement in understanding. Pupils who reverse or omit parts of sentences will find it difficult to make sense of mathematics text. Small words are often missed when reading, but these small words are often essential in mathematics. Many pupils ask their teachers continually, 'What do I have to do now?' which may be a result of their reading problems.

*Teachers may help by:*

- Talking about mathematics using correct terminology during problem solving sessions.

- Employing a 'reading for meaning' approach, encouraging the pupil to *expect* the text to make sense.

- Encouraging a graphical or pictorial approach and spending time discussing the outcomes.

- Providing reading lists of essential words and using whatever method is being used to teach reading to help the pupil learn them.

- Encouraging pupils to highlight the important parts of written questions.

## Naming difficulties

Some otherwise able pupils are unable to name signs and symbols correctly. Or naming is sometimes correct, sometimes not. This difficulty is often apparent in their oral work. These pupils will be able to copy an exercise and carry out a mathematics task correctly but will misread aloud what they have written. Incorrect oral answers may be given, misleading the teacher about their ability. Many pupils with SpLD will also have difficulty remembering terms such as 'diagonal', 'perimeter', 'area', 'radius', 'diameter' and 'circumference' and naming cylinders, spheres, cuboids and other solid shapes.

*Teachers will help by:*

- Giving genuine praise to pupils for understanding the mathematics.

- Not focusing undue attention on this type of error.

- Presenting a variety of learning situations that invite pupils to extract the meaning.

- Providing illustrated mathematics dictionaries (these can be compiled by individual pupils).

- Assisting conceptualisation when possible by the presentation of several concrete examples.

## Writing difficulties

Many pupils show a well-developed sense of mathematics and are able to engage successfully in oral and practical lessons. Their problems become apparent when answers must be written down. Single digits and letters are reversed, tens and units are reversed, spelling is bizarre and page layout is chaotic with many crossings out.

Some of the writing difficulties parallel those seen in other language-based subjects. Giving written expression to ideas is likely to cause problems.

*Teachers will help by:*

- Addressing the mechanics, ie correct posture, pen-hold and pen movement.

- Encouraging correct use of ruler and other drawing and measuring instruments.

- Helping pupils clarify their thinking and select the correct format for recording their ideas and solutions to problems.

- Encouraging the use of a rough jotter for mathematical 'doodling' before writing the solution neatly in its final form.

## Organisational difficulties

These may manifest in untidy page layout, difficulties in keeping files/books in order, frequent loss of stationery and equipment, and poor time management.

The causes may be poor memory, spatial and temporal sequencing difficulties, and possibly emotional factors.

*Teachers will help by:*

- Giving direct instructions about page layout and checking pupils' work early in the lesson to make sure the instructions are being carried out.

- Providing sample layouts for individual use.

- Insisting that all drawing is done in pencil and all lines drawn with a ruler.

- Providing squared paper and insisting that each square is occupied by a single digit. Because of memory problems these instructions will need to be repeated frequently, possibly several times per lesson.

- Allowing adequate time for neat work, making sure that one task is completed before moving on to the next.

**Emotional difficulties**

Many pupils feel anxious about mathematics. Showing their difficulties publicly is particularly feared. If these fears intensify and accumulate, they may manifest themselves in avoidance behaviours, such as doing their work very slowly in the hope that the lesson will finish before their inadequacies become apparent. In extreme cases, absence from school through psychosomatic sickness or truancy may also be a mathematics avoidance behaviour.

*Teachers will help by:*

- Avoiding asking SpLD pupils to answer direct questions in open class, or say their tables aloud with other pupils listening.

- Creating opportunities for collaborative working where their contribution can be valued.

- Seeing that tasks set are within the capacity of the student to perform and that where help is likely to be needed, the help is organised and available.

- Explaining the situation and the pupil's coping strategies to his or her parent(s) or carer.

- Planning for success.

**The need for over-learning**

Because of memory problems, pupils with SpLD tend to require revision more frequently than their peers. The 1995 National Curriculum Orders allow for and encourage frequent revisiting. The accompanying curriculum planning guidance documents (SCAA, *Planning the Curriculum at Key Stages 1 and 2*, 1995) demonstrate ways in which this may be managed.

*Teachers will help by:*

- Ensuring that all equipment matches the social interest and intellectual maturity level of the pupil. In some circumstances even 'neutral' material such as Cuisenaire rods must be used with sensitivity with older pupils.

- Ensuring examples of work from an earlier Key Stage are commensurate with their chronological age.

- Ensuring that revisited topics are presented in new contexts and are not just a rehash of previous work.

**Conclusion**

Each pupil with SpLD will present a different pattern of difficulties and abilities. It is likely that more than one aspect of the overall problem can be dealt with simultaneously, eg a disorganised approach and the need to understand place value for decimal fractions. However, it will be necessary to establish priorities in terms of helping the pupil to cope with some of the mathematics being carried out by his or her classmates and ensuring that vital prenumber and early stage knowledge are put in place.

Most important, however, is that the teacher's attitude be positive, cheerful and encouraging so that pupils feel their abilities and personal qualities are appreciated. If pupils feel valued, they will respond.

# Chapter 4 – An Individualised Programme

**About the programme**

Individualisation means that the programme has been constructed as a planned sequence of suitably selected lessons and activities and to present teaching and learning situations that are most appropriate to the assessed needs of the individual. It offers the pupil opportunity to learn in the classroom, through differentiated class activities, large and small group work, and individual work. It cannot be overemphasised that we must clearly differentiate between an *individualised* programme, tailored to the needs of the individual and often carried out in a class or group situation, and an *individual* programme which assumes one-to-one teaching. *An individualised **learning** programme is not an individual **teaching** programme.*

The increased flexibility of the revised National Curriculum Orders (DfE 1995) makes it possible for teachers to plan individualised programmes that include material across the Key Stage, and where necessary from other Key Stages, without the need for disapplication or modification. They should, therefore, be planned to include National Curriculum programmes of study.

The following case study illustrates an individualised programme of study for a particular pupil, Peter. His programme was selected because his learning difficulties (see page 31) are characteristics of pupils with SpLD in both primary and secondary schools. It is classroom-based and linked to mathematics in the National Curriculum. The programme is concerned with the development of Peter's knowledge, understanding and skills, with particular attention being given to his specific learning difficulties. The programme is both progressive and cumulative, and has been planned to fit into the school's mathematics curriculum, which in turn took guidance from *Planning the Curriculum at Key Stages 1 and 2* (SCAA, 1995). Hence the choice of a single progressive programme in preference to a collection of curriculum items. This particular programme fits into the number section of the school's curriculum. The notional time allowed for number in the school concerned is two hours per week.

It must be stressed that this is **not** the full extent of the mathematics curriculum for this pupil; it is only the number section. This is the area identified when the IEP was prepared at Stage 2 of the *Code of Practice.*

Pre-programme assessment indicated that Peter was in need of a programme that revisited Key Stage 1 of the National Curriculum and included AT 2 Number offering it at a faster pace, with age neutral examples:

3  (a)    use repeating patterns to develop ideas of regularity and sequencing;

    (b)    explore and record patterns in addition and subtraction, and then patterns of multiples, *eg 3, 6, 9, 12,* explaining their pattern and using them to make predictions; progress to exploring further patterns involving multiplication and division, including those within a hundred-square of multiplication facts;

    (c)    know addition and subtraction facts to twenty, and develop a range of mental methods for finding, from known facts, those that they cannot recall; learn multiplication and division facts relating to 2s, 5s, 10s, and use these to learn other facts, eg *double multiples of 2 to produce multiples of 4,* and to develop mental methods for finding new results;

    (d)    develop a variety of methods for adding and subtracting, including using the fact that subtraction is the inverse of addition;

    (e)    use a basic calculator, reading the display, *eg use the constant function to explore repeated addition.*

Time for 'rehearsal' of earlier material had been built into the school's curriculum, enabling other pupils (without IEPs) to work collaboratively with Peter to strengthen their number facts skills.

The classroom teacher, who had recently attended a course on special needs in mathematics, was able to manage the delivery of the programme herself. Support from the special educational needs co-ordinator (SENCO) and external agencies was in the form of teacher advice. If teachers elect for direct pupil support from a specialist teacher, then it is important that the input is carefully planned and co-ordinated to maximise the effective use of that support teacher.

The outcome of any successful learning programme depends on what the pupil brings to each new learning situation. Pupils with SpLD have their own often unique set of learning problems. Their programmes need to move with them and therefore *cannot* be planned against a list of skill hierarchies (see page 37).

Although the area of concern in Peter's mathematical development was identified as written and remembered number facts, the teacher was well aware of the effect that the irregular pace and interest diversion of pupils with SpLD in mathematics have on an over-prescriptive programme. Individualisation means moving with the pupil and therefore programmes should be planned to match the changing needs of the pupil and support him or her in accessing the school curriculum.

## An Example of an Individualised Programme
## A Programme for Peter

The following information was gathered from the variety of assessment procedures given in Chapter 2 of this book.

### Assessment

### Performance

Name: Peter     Age: 9 years 4 months

Positive:      Sound discrimination and sound blending are good (reading skills).

            Good use of coping strategies. Ability to recognise patterns; logic and reasoning good.

Difficulties:   Weak short-term memory, both auditory sequential and visual sequential. Letters and digits are reversed and often sentences are not in sequence.

            Poor understanding of place value and understanding of symbols is weak. His linking of real situations to symbols very weak.

To sum up the assessment of Peter's overall performance in mathematics, it was noted that items on the test that were in meaningful context or followed a logical pattern were within his grasp. The rest seemed to be a jumbled mass of unrelated symbols.

### Background information

Peter dislikes maths, finding it complicated, confusing and awkward. His level of frustration is high.

Peter was working within the programme of study for his Key Stage (KS 2) but had forgotten much of his earlier work. His dislike of mathematics made it necessary to rebuild his self-confidence, which meant that extra care had to be taken to see that his work was age-neutral and that suitable class/group activities formed the core of his programme.

### *Planning the programme*
Selecting the content

It was decided by the class teacher and the SENCO that Peter needed to 'revisit' the programme of study for Key Stage 1 of the National Curriculum for further work on number facts to 20 (KS 1, Number, 3 (c)):

> know addition and subtraction facts to 20, and develop a range of mental methods for finding, from known facts, those that they cannot recall; learn multiplication and division facts relating to 2s, 5s, 10s, and use these to learn other facts, *eg double multiples of 2 to produce multiples of 4,* and to develop mental methods for finding new results.

Selecting the context

The way forward was seen as teaching him through his preferred learning style:

- working at a semantic/meaningful level by converting 'sums' into everyday practical problems;

- using patterns to help him understand the structure of mathematics;

- devising strategies to overcome his poor reading skills.

This was to be presented through individualised work within a classroom setting. Work was to be differentiated to provide equality of opportunity for Peter to access the school curriculum.

Organising the work
  Medium term

  When considering Peter's programme alongside her medium-term plan for the whole class, the class teacher decided to classify the work into three stages:

    Stage 1: Addition facts to ten
    Stage 2: Subtraction facts to ten
    Stage 3: Number facts to twenty

  Short term

  The class teacher wished to follow a pupil-orientated programme and therefore needed flexibility to move with her pupil. Although the three 'stages' identified in the medium-term plan could be broken down into smaller steps, she felt that this could prove detrimental to the flexibility of the programme. Her medium-term plan and continuous teacher assessment ensured that her programme would remain purposeful.

*An over-prescriptive programme often inhibits teachers from responding to relevant enrichment items suggested by individual pupils* (see page 31).

Pupil involvement

The teacher explained to Peter that she thought that he had forgotten some of his earlier work and that she would like him to 'revisit' previous work using new methods to help him remember.

Peter agreed to a programme based on earlier work involving number facts to ten and comprising class/group work.

Parental involvement

Peter's parents were informed of his IEP and consequently agreed to support him at home when requested.

## STAGE 1: Addition facts to ten
### *Establishing an appropriate starting point*

In order to establish an appropriate starting point for Peter his class teacher needed to know his present state of knowledge and understanding of addition facts to ten. She presented him with the following task:

Individual

Peter was presented with ten Smarties and asked to arrange them in any way he wished.

He immediately placed them in two sets of five. When asked to record this in his book he wrote:

$$5 + 1$$

When asked to explain what he had written he pointed to the first group and said, 'That's one five,' then pointed to the other set and said, 'That's another five'. His understanding of the concept was clear but he did not know how to record the result.

Peter needed his programme to provide a wide variety of experience in connecting concrete examples to their symbolic representation. This would be an appropriate starting point.

### *Following the programme (Stage 1)*

Number at the connecting level (addition to ten)

To make it easier for the reader to follow Peter's progress within his individualised programme, all of his spoken and active responses have been written in ***bold italics***.

1. Activity (large group/class)

Many children who have difficulty with number at the connecting level would benefit from the following activity, which can be used as a reinforcement and revision exercise. In Peter's class this type of visualisation was a common feature in the mathematics programme. It must be remembered that mathematics does not have to be difficult for children to be learning.

Teacher:    *Wrote number 5 on the board.*
            'Look at the number and tell me what you see in your mind. I see five ducks.'
Pupil 1:    'I see five plates on a table.'
Teacher:    'Does anyone see anything different?'
Pupil 2:    'I see five monkeys in a tree.'

This activity continued for as long as it was interesting to the children. In Peter's programme it was necessary to ensure that during the activity he had been encouraged to contribute his visualisation, which was, *'I see five trees in a garden.'*

Teacher:    *Extended the symbols to read 5 + 2.*
            'What can you see now?'
Pupil 1:    'I can see five boys and two girls.'
Teacher:    'Can anyone see anything different?'
Pupil 2:    'I can see five red crayons and two blue ones.'

Once again the activity continued until Peter had contributed and the answers ceased to come. Peter's answer was, *'I can see five bikes and two cars.'*

Teacher:     *Cleared the board and asked for volunteers to write the following statements on the board in symbols:*
'4 oranges and 2apples.'
'6 girls and 2 boys.'
'5 Smarties and 5 Smarties' *inviting Peter to do this one.*

NB   Answers were not required at this stage. Here pupils were making transference from visualisation of reality situations through verbal communications to symbols.

2. Activities (small group)

There were four other children within Peter's class who benefited from the following activities and although we are following Peter's progress, the inclusion of other children led to valuable discussion at pupil level (see page 9).

Pupils were each given two small plastic bags and the + written on card. *Peter was asked if he knew what the sign + meant. He knew it meant 'and' but could not give any other word for the process.* Pupils within the group contributed 'add' and 'plus'. These words were then written on the backs of the cards displaying the + sign. The pupils were asked to share the ten Smarties between their two bags in as many different ways as they could think of. *Peter quickly grasped the idea and started by placing two in one bag and eight in the other. He then placed the + sign between them and said, 'Two and eight'. Peter soon stopped putting Smarties into the bag and just placed them on the top.*

3. Discussion and recording (small group)

The children within the group were asked to record their results in symbols. *Through group discussion Peter was able to supply the answers without teacher intervention.*

At this stage the = sign was introduced. *Peter did not know what it meant, but when he heard the word 'equals' he said that he had heard the word before. He did know that the non-equivalent sets that he had recorded so far must add up to ten because that was the total number of Smarties. He recorded the results of his investigation in maths symbols with ease.*

4. Investigation (individual/group)

The group proceeded with this activity and *Peter commented that, 'There's loads of ways if you cut them in half as well.' He also discovered the commutative law of addition saying, 'Oh, you can turn them the other way round.' From then on he abandoned the use of the Smarties and simply recorded the reverse of what he had done previously.*

*Having discovered the commutative law of addition he then reinforced it by assisting his peers in their understanding. This was an invaluable motivator.*

5. Reinforcement (addition to ten) (large group)

The group was then asked to carry out a series of investigations and activities to add variety and breadth to the initial concept. At this point it was appropriate to include a further group of five children who, although they had no difficulty recording number facts, were experiencing difficulty with instant recall. The visual/kinaesthetic approach to the following investigation was appropriate to all and the discussion between group members added both auditory and spoken experience.

The group were asked to record their addition facts on a peg board using two different coloured pegs.

*Peter began laboriously, placing out one red and then counting out the blue as he put them in the board. He did this for three rows and then, recognising the pattern, carried on without counting. He was able to predict the number of pegs needed in each row 'because the blues go down one every time'.*

*He recorded the pattern in his book and wrote the digits in the appropriate margin thus, transferring from the concrete to the abstract as a result of practical experience and real understanding (Figure 8).*

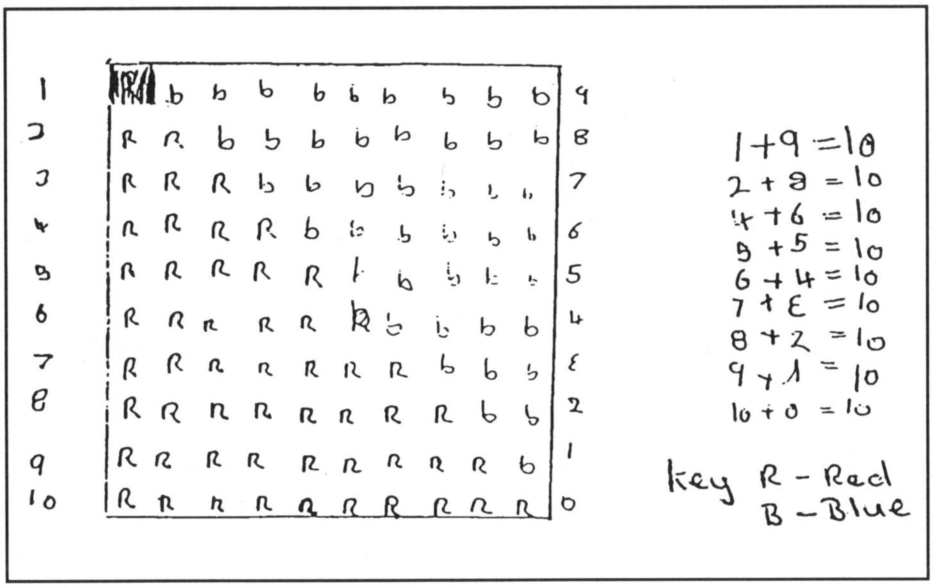

Figure 8.

All this was carried out in a group situation where mathematical discussion promoted the development of reason and logical thinking.

## 6. Activity (whole class)

The following game was selected to extend Peter's memory of number facts to ten. When differentiated it was useful to all other members of the class for both memory extension of number facts and mental addition.

The pelmanism game was played as a whole class activity; each group of four children had a set of cards which were blank on one side and had numbers on the other side. The objective was to turn over two blank cards with digits on their reverse to make a given number. The total number was graded according to the ability of the individuals within each group. *Peter's group had to find two cards whose numbers when added together made ten. Peter's confidence was greatly boosted when he was able to predict correctly which card was needed and eventually win the game.*

## 7. Activity (teacher-led)

*To reinforce and make Peter's knowledge of addition facts to ten automatic. He was asked to make a strip of ten multilink cubes.* The teacher placed the strip behind her back, broke off a section and showed the children that section only. She asked them to tell her how many were still behind her back. *Peter found it necessary, after counting the number shown, to use his fingers to count on. He felt that this was 'babyish' and tried to hide his fingers under his desk. The teacher showed him how to make tally marks instead,* and to give everyone equal opportunity to answer at their own speed she asked children to write down their answers and keep them hidden until everyone had an answer.

## 8. Activity (parent or carer)
*Peter's parents supported him by repeating this activity at home, on a daily basis, until he became more fluent.*

## 9. Activity (group)
The child with SpLD needs a great deal of practice and over-learning in order to internalise facts. With this in mind Peter's teacher included number facts pattern activities in the programme for his group. These began with number facts patterns to five using a 25-pin geoboard and elastic bands. The pupils had made their own geoboards during a technology lesson by placing 'dotted' paper onto offcuts of wood and hammering nails into the dots covering a 5 x 5 square.

## 10. Exposition (teacher)
The teacher numbered the nails along the vertical and horizontal axes with the numbers 0, 1, 2, 3 and 4 and demonstrated that by linking number 4 on the vertical axis to number 1 on the horizontal axis, with an elastic band, it would give the numbers 4 and 1. If this was in turn made into an addition sum 4 + 1 the answer would be five. She then asked the children to work together and see how many pairs of numbers they could link together to make five.

## 11. Multisensory activity (group)
The children talked about their patterns (auditory), joined pairs of pins with different coloured elastic bands (kinaesthetic) and saw a pattern evolve (visual), then recorded the results (motor) *(Figure 9)*.

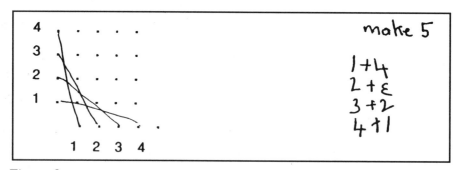

*Figure 9.*

*Peter commented on the fact that the 0 pin did not have any elastic bands on it.* A group discussion on the zero ensued:

| | |
|---|---|
| Pupil 1: | 'Try it with the four.' |
| Pupil 2: | 'Four and nothing doesn't make five, you can't do it.' |
| Peter: | *'It's like the Smarties, they're like two groups that make five, one and four make five.'* (Now he was linking the experience with items stored in his long-term memory, an important development for Peter.) |

Peter was making the link through something that was pleasant to him, ie Smarties. Children who have memory problems are often able to store facts in their long-term memories, and retrieve them on cue, if the facts are linked to something pleasurable to the child.

| | |
|---|---|
| Teacher: | 'What would you need to put with the zero to make five?' |
| Peter: | *'Four Smarties in one bag and one in the other, that makes five. So if you get nothing in one bag you must get five in the other.'* (Here he was using logic; one of his identified strengths.) |

| Teacher: | (building on his strengths) 'Does it only work with Smarties?' |
| Pupil: | 'No, it can work with anything, like when we closed our eyes and saw things the other day.' (Visualisation, used earlier in the programme – see page 33.) |
| Teacher: | 'OK, what do you see when I say zero and three?' |
| Pupil: | 'I see no fish and three chips?' |
| Teacher: | 'Can you see "no fish"?' |

A discussion ensued resulting in Peter concluding with, *'No, you can only see the three chips, we could really just say three chips.'*

| Teacher: | 'If I said no fish and nine chips, what would you see then?' |
| Group response: | 'Nine chips.' |
| Teacher: | 'How would you write that? Show me.' |

The group discussed this relating it to the visualisation activity on page 33 and finally wrote $0 + 9$.

| Teacher: | 'Who can write the answer?' |
| *She selected Peter who wrote $0 + 9 = 9$.* | |
| Teacher: | 'Make some more of your own zero sums.' |

This type of spontaneous questioning cannot be indicated in a prescriptive IEP. It is difficult to say exactly where a pupil-orientated programme in mathematics will lead both teacher and learner, therefore it is advisable not to stick rigidly to a programme that has generated from a check-list of hierarchical skills (see Denvir, *Understanding of number concepts in low attaining 7 – 9 year olds,* 1986). When planning programmes for pupils with SpLD, careful consideration needs to be given to the amount of time indicated for the duration of each step. Leave plenty of time for discussion.

The pupils produced further examples of addition using zero, then read aloud what they had written and made 'number stories' to match the symbols.

12. Activity (whole class)

Peter's teacher considered this an appropriate time to 'rehearse' number facts with the whole class. She produced a laminated number line for numbers 0 to 20, which initially she folded in half to display the numbers 0 to 10.

Peter's group was invited to demonstrate their number stories on the line.

*Peter said, 'I went fishing and caught three big fish and no little fish. Show me!'*
*He then invited his friend to come and demonstrate the 'sum' on the number line.*

Many children demonstrated number stories that did not contain a zero, thus putting the activity into perspective.

The children were enthusiastic about the activity and so the teacher extended the number line to include numbers 11 to 20. (Pupils had thus directed the programme beyond its planned parameters.)

*Peter was able to make the transference to larger numbers.*

13. Investigation (individual/group)

The group was then asked to extend the geoboard investigation to include addition facts to twenty. After some discussion, they decided to disregard the geoboard and went straight ahead with recording (*Figure 10*). They extended the activity to include further examples of their own. *Peter's examples are shown in Figures 11, 12 and 13.*

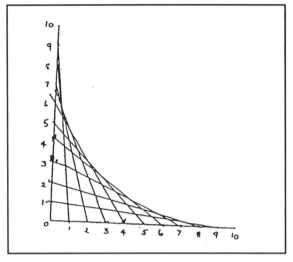

Figure 10.

Figure 11.

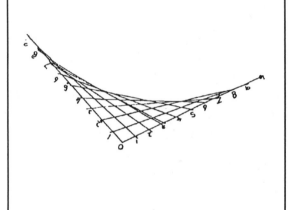

Figure 12.

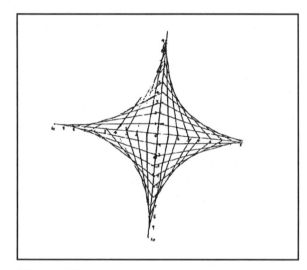

Figure 13.

The teacher encouraged her pupils to make use of the vocabulary for addition by reading their patterns in as many different ways as they could think of: 9 add 1 equals 10, 8 plus 2 equals 10, the total of 7 and 3 is 10, the sum of 6 and 4 is 10, 5 and 5 is 10.

14. Investigation (parent or carer)
*Peter made further parabolic patterns at home and brought them into school the following day.*

15. Differentiated activities (whole class)
While Peter's group were involved with their number patterns, other groups within the class were finding number patterns in bonds to twenty, and in multiplication tables. The teacher gave support to each of the groups in turn.

### Assessment of progress (Stage 1)
Here the teacher faced a dilemma. Should she assess only what she had set out to teach, ie addition facts to ten, or, should she assess other items that had been introduced in order to enrich the programme, ie use of an addition line to twenty?

This perplexes many teachers who are following an individualised programme, particularly if the items are identified in another 'stage' of the IEP. Two important points to consider are:

1. Who is being assessed, the pupil or the teacher?
2. Can we predict what a child is going to learn?

Peter's teacher (rightly or wrongly) decided to assess his progress with addition facts to ten at this point, and to assess his proficiency in addition facts to twenty at the beginning of Stage 3 of the programme.

a) Accuracy of symbolic recording
Assessment of Peter's progress was achieved simply by asking him to put out two lots of five Smarties and record what he had done (he could not do this at the start of his programme, see page 33). He wrote 5 + 5 without hesitation. Several further assessment questions were asked to make sure that this was not just a 'one off' situation. He correctly recorded them all.

b) Recall of addition facts
To assess his ability to recall addition facts to ten Peter's teacher asked him to supply the answers to a series of number fact questions. She noted that he gave the correct answer to all number facts with a total no greater than five and all 'doubles' (3 + 3, 2 + 2 etc). She concluded that the visualisation activities had helped him to recall images of numbers within his visual range, ie one to five and that his ability to see patterns helped him to remember the 'doubles'. She made a note that she would use this information when planning future work for Peter.

*Outcome of assessment of progress*
Although Peter was not able to recall all addition facts to ten, he had made marked progress. His weak short-term memory could prevent him from ever being able to remember and recall all number facts. His teacher hoped that frequent 'rehearsal' of this work would increase progress.

Peter had mastered symbolic recording of addition facts to ten. It was time to progress to Stage 2.

## STAGE 2: Subtraction facts to ten
### Establishing an appropriate starting point
Since symbolism was an area of difficulty for Peter, the teacher needed to spend time assessing the extent of the problem before continuing with his programme.

Individual
Peter's teacher showed him the subtraction sign. He knew this as 'take away'. She then asked him to take six Smarties away from ten. He counted orally as he removed them. When she asked how many were left he found it necessary to count and gave the correct answer. He was not using instant recall, or linking the situation to previous activities in order to find a solution, a difficulty noted in his profile. It was interesting to note that in the previous step of his programme (addition facts to ten) he did manage to link work with previous experience. This inconsistency (here today, gone tomorrow, back again on Thursday) with the retrieval of facts from long-term memory is characteristic of many pupils with SpLD.

In order to assess his ability to convert from the concrete to the abstract, the teacher asked him to record what he had done. He wrote:

$$6 - 10 = 4$$

Teacher:     'Can you explain that to me?'
Peter:       *'Yes, six from ten is four.'*

He was recording the operation in the order in which he had done it which seemed perfectly logical to him. It was necessary to explain to him the convention of placing the larger number first. It did occur to his teacher that perhaps he assumed that the commutative law for addition also applied to subtraction. She then checked to see if other children were under the same misapprehension and found that several of them were.

Peter's programme would start with symbolic recording of subtraction facts.

### Following the programme (Stage 2)

Number at the connecting level (subtraction to ten)

1. Activity (small group)

The teacher grouped together six children who also had difficulty with recording subtraction. She elected not to use Smarties this time as children needed to realise that this was not just a Smarties situation. She put out a selection of plastic bottle tops, multilink cubes and paper clips, but before any concrete representation was made she returned to her visualisation method.

Teacher:     'Close your eyes and picture five ice lollies. Now watch two of them melt. How
             many do you have left?'
Pupil response:    'Three.'
Teacher:     'Draw that for me, please.'(*Figure 14*)
**Peter's response:**

*Figure 14.*

At this point the teacher showed her pupils a card with the subtraction sign on it and asked them what it was called. Most of the children knew it as 'take away', but one child was able to add 'subtract' and 'minus'. The teacher explained that the subtraction sign went after the five to tell them that they were going to take some away. Because two lollies had melted they would need to take two away, therefore,

$$5 - 2 = 3$$

The teacher offered several further examples, each time representing the reality items with the apparatus, eg there were five children and three ran away, show me. (See *Investigations and Problem Solving*, El-Naggar, 1995.) Children recorded their results. Finally, the teacher returned to the example relating to children.

Teacher:     'Five children; which number will I show for five children?'
Peter:       *'Is it five?'*
Teacher:     'Come and write that on the board, Peter.'
Teacher:     'If three of them ran away, how many will be left?'
Pupils:      'Two.'

Pupils were encouraged to make up their own number stories and record them in symbol. They could use apparatus including a number line if they wished to do so.

The teacher drew the attention of her pupils to the 'children' example by drawing it on the board *(Figure 15)*.

*Figure 15.*

| | |
|---|---|
| Teacher: | 'What would happen if the children came back?' |
| Pupils: | 'You would have five again.' |
| Teacher: | 'How would we write that?' |
| Peter: | *'You would put them ... like, you would put the two and three, that would make the five again.'* |
| Teacher: | 'Could you write that for me?' |

Peter wrote:

$$5 - 3 = 2$$
$$2 + 3 = 5$$

| | |
|---|---|
| Teacher: | 'Can you read that to me, Peter?' |
| Peter: | *'Five take away three makes two, and two and three makes five.'* |
| Teacher: | 'Very good, Peter. Can anyone read it another way?' |
| Pupil 1: | 'Five minus three equals two, and two plus three equals five.' |
| Teacher: | 'Is there another way?' |
| Pupil 2: | 'Yes, five subtract three makes two, and two add three makes five.' |
| Teacher: | 'Well done.' |

*Peter saw the relationship between the numbers, discovering that subtraction is the inverse of addition. He then went on to look at examples with other numbers within the range of one to ten. Peter reinforced his own concepts by explaining the inverse facility to other members of his group.*

2. Activity (large group)

The class teacher drew together nineteen children (including Peter) who needed to 'rehearse' number facts. *She asked Peter to demonstrate the relationship between addition and subtraction, which he enjoyed.* She then invited volunteers to suggest further examples. After each example, the pupils recorded the results in their books.

When the children were responding appropriately to numbers to ten, she extended the work to include numbers to twenty.

*Peter found this work comparatively easy and was able to concentrate on correct number formation.*

### Assessment of progress (Stage 2)

Once again Peter's teacher made the decision to assess only his progress in subtraction facts to ten. Assessment of his ability with numbers to twenty would be made at the beginning of Stage 3 of his programme.

a) Accuracy of symbolic recording

In order to assess Peter's progress in symbolic recording, his class teacher returned to the example with which he had difficulty at the onset of his programme, ie 'Take six Smarties away from ten' (see page 39). This time he placed the numbers in correct order:

$$10 - 6 = 4$$

Several further assessment questions were asked to make sure that this was not just a 'one off' situation and although he made a couple of mistakes he was able to correct them himself.

b) Recall of subtraction facts

When asked to supply the answers to a number of addition fact questions (both 'verbal' and 'written'), he was less confident than he had been with addition facts. He used visualisation for the smaller numbers and his fingers for the larger ones. He was more successful with written questions because he did not have to hold the numbers in his mind while he solved the problem (short-term memory problem).

### Outcome of assessment of progress

Peter had made progress in symbolic recording of subtraction facts to ten, but needed constant 'rehearsal' in this area.

Accurate, spontaneous recall of number facts was still weak, but Peter could use his own strategies to solve subtraction problems to ten. Peter's memory problem (indicated in his initial assessment, page 31) indicated that he would always find spontaneous recall difficult, and as he had adequate skills and concepts to enable him to solve subtraction problems it was decided to move on in his programme. It is through constant practice that number facts eventually become spontaneous, therefore Peter's parents were approached about providing him with practice at home. They agreed to help him with homework provided by the class teacher.

### STAGE 3: Number facts to twenty
### Establishing an appropriate starting point

Assessment of addition and subtraction facts to twenty was through direct questioning and observation of recording. All but a few of Peter's answers were derived through a mixture of visualisation and the use of a number line, the exception being 'doubles' which he could recall spontaneously. There were frequent number reversals with 14, 15, 16, 17 and 18, even when he copied them from the number line.

In order to plan the next stage in Peter's programme it was important to build on his successes from the previous two stages. Peter had been successful in remembering number facts relating to 'doubles', therefore his teacher used this fact as a starting point in the assessment of his competence with equal addition and then multiplication.

Individual

The number of Smarties was increased to twenty. Not forgetting to satisfy Peter's sense of taste, the teacher gave him a few Smarties to eat.

Teacher:    'Put out two lots of five Smarties, Peter.'
*Peter put out two sets each containing five Smarties.*
Teacher:    'Can you write that down for me, Peter?'
Peter:      *'Yes.' He proceeded to write 5 + 5 = 10.*
Teacher:    'Well done, now can you add another lot of five Smarties to make three 'lots' or 'sets' of Smarties?'

*Peter placed another set of five Smarties on the table.*

Teacher:    'How many Smarties do you have now?'

Peter:      *'Fifteen.'*

Teacher:    'Can you write that for me?'

*He wrote 5 + 5 + 5.*

Teacher:    'How many 5s do you have?'

Peter:      *'Three.'*

Teacher:    'Can you write that in another way?'

Peter:      *'Three lots of five.'*

Teacher:    'Do you know the sign for 'lots of'?'

As he wrote he asked, *'Is it x? Ah, if I put x instead of "lots of", is that it?'*

Teacher:    'BINGO!'

*Peter was encouraged by the delight expressed by his teacher and wrote 3 x 5.*

Teacher:    'Now add one more lot of five to the group of Smarties. How many lots are there? Write it down.'

*He began to write 4 lots of 5 and then crossed it out and said, 'Oh it's easier to write 4 x 5.'*

Teacher:    'How many Smarties are there?'

Peter:      *'Twenty – it's easy, 'cos it's ten and ten.'*


The teacher concluded his assessment by drawing on Peter's ability to use pattern and asked him to add up in fives. He did this with confidence. She then wrote 7 x 5 and asked if he could supply the answer. He used his fingers to keep count as he went up in fives but went too far. His short-term memory was finding difficulty in coping with two activities simultaneously. The next step in his programme would start with making a multiplication table and learning how to use it. This would be laminated and he would be encouraged to carry it with him and make frequent use of it.

Many children in Peter's class found multiplication facts difficult and the teacher decided that the whole class would benefit from a series of activities related to multiplication. Differentiation would be through teacher intervention and enrichment activities.


## Following the programme (Stage 3)

Making a multiplication square


1. a) Exposition by the teacher (whole class)

The teacher used an overhead projector to show examples of an addition ready reckoner and a hundred-square multiplication ready reckoner and gave an explanation as to how they worked. This opened discussion on their usefulness in the days of the electronic calculator, but they all said that they would like to make one (some for their siblings).


b) Activity (groups)

Each child was given a sheet of squared paper and invited to make an 11 x 11 square. They were then asked to follow the model displayed on the OHP and place an x in the bottom left-hand square. Putting the origin in the bottom left-hand corner rather than in the top left corner prepares pupils for work on co-ordinates and graphs *(Figure 17)*.

Several pupils (including Peter) found this difficult and were given a 5 x 5 square to start with *(Figure 16)*. When they understood how this functioned they transferred their 5 x 5 squares onto an 11 x 11 square and continued with the class activity.

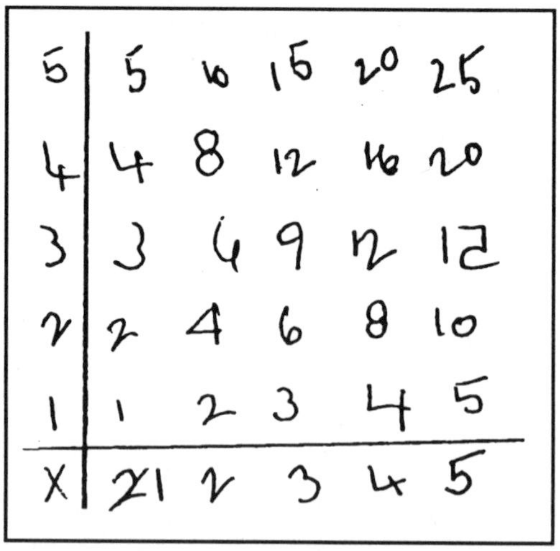

Figure 16.

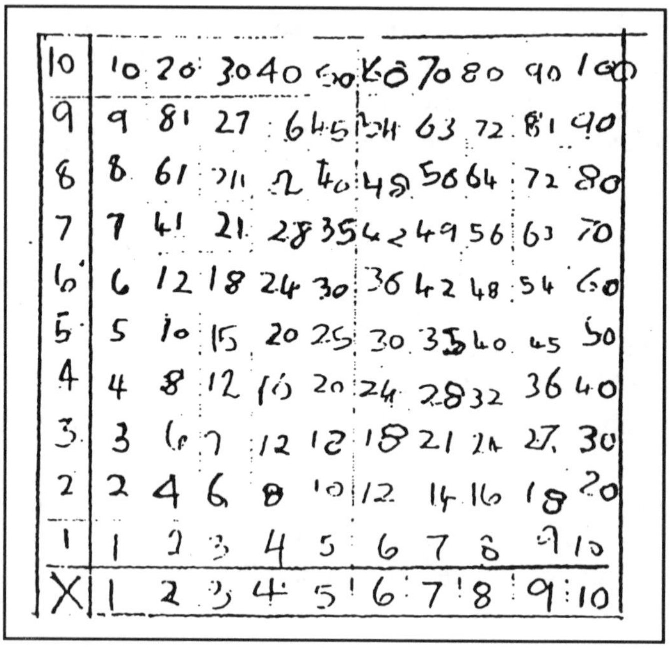

Figure 17.

c) Individual

*Peter's teacher asked him to use his calculator to generate the numbers in the seven times table and check them against his own. He noticed his mistake with 14, and then realised that 16 and 18 were also incorrectly written, but before he corrected them his teacher spent some time with him talking about their values. He understood the values, it had been a symbolic mistake and therefore it could be approached at the symbolic stage.*

*His teacher gave him a 10 x 10 grid and asked him to insert the numbers 1 to 10 in the top row, beginning in the top left-hand square. When he had completed that, she asked him to continue writing the numbers in the next row beginning with 11 and saying them aloud as he went – 'One ten and one, one ten and two, one ten and three' etc. in order to avoid the error made in the table square.*

2. a) Activity (whole class)

To add variety to the teaching approach to reinforcement and revision of tables, the teacher showed the whole class part of Carol Vorderman's *Video Class, Times Tables*. For teachers who have not seen the video: It is a highly motivating video designed to help children to remember

44

tables. It uses a multisensory approach, *auditory* through singing the tables to 'pop' music, *visual* approach through visual effects, and *kinaesthetic* through dancing and finger patterns.

## b) Parent or carer

The children really enjoyed this activity and the teacher lent a copy to Peter, for him to use at home, where he could stop and rewind the tape whenever he wanted to do so. His parents reported that they had learnt a thing or two about multiplication tables, as well as Peter.

## 3. a) Activities (whole class)

When discussing the Vorderman video many of the children said that they had found the items on multiplication table patterns very interesting. As a follow-up the teacher put out a selection of activities at various 'number stations' around the classroom. There were calculator games, computer programmes for generating number patterns, work cards for use with structured apparatus, and paper and pencil activities.

The teacher explained that during the next few days she wanted each child to attempt at least one activity from each 'station'. She left the exact timing open to enable enrichment or early closure of the activities as needed.

*Peter was confused by the wide variety of items on offer (pupils with SpLD often have this problem) and wandered about not doing anything in particular. He clearly needed some help.*

## b) Individual work

The teacher asked him to write down his two times table, with the aid of either his multiplication square or a calculator. *He chose his multiplication square and successfully wrote his two times table to 10 x 2.*

His teacher then asked him if he could see a pattern in it. *He remembered the pattern on the tape, in the units column of the answers: 0, 2, 4, 6, 8, 0, 2, 4, 6, 8 repeated.* The teacher gave Peter a ten-point circle and asked him to join the dots according to the pattern of the two times table (*Figure 18*).

Ten-point circles

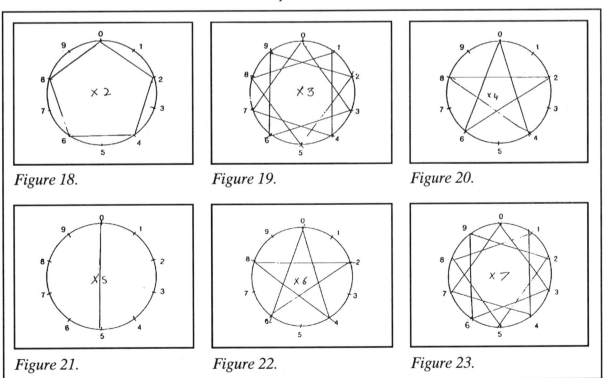

| Figure 18. | Figure 19. | Figure 20. |

| Figure 21. | Figure 22. | Figure 23. |

*Peter went on to discover and record any similar patterns in the multiplication tables one to seven (Figures 19, 20, 21, 22, 23). He enjoyed this investigation and went to work with two of his friends who were looking for patterns in a hundred squares.*

c) Reinforcement (parent or carer)

*Peter took some of the multiplication activities home and his parents helped him with them.*

4. Division facts (individual)

Back to the twenty Smarties!

Teacher: 'When you have sweets I'm sure you share them with your friends, Peter.'

Peter: *'Sometimes.'*

Teacher: 'Well, we're going to share these Smarties. I want you to share the Smarties between you and me.'

Peter: *'That's easy, ten each.' He counted out ten and separated them from the rest.*

The teacher took advantage of the situation and asked him to record what he had done. He wrote:

$$10 + 10$$

Teacher: 'What are you doing?'

Peter: *'Sharing.'*

Teacher: 'Do you know what sign we use for sharing?'

Peter: *'Not really.'*

His teacher gave him a card with the ÷ sign on. He looked at it and said, *'Oh, it's the one I don't know.'*

Teacher: 'Let's use it. You started with twenty Smarties, so write down 20. Now write the sign for sharing. How many were sharing? Write that down next.'

*By now he was writing 20 ÷ 2.*

Teacher: 'Can you finish the sum yourself?'

*He wrote the equals sign and the answer. He did it correctly.*

On the back of the card with the division sign on, the teacher wrote the word divide, and asked Peter to say the other word for division. Peter then made sums to show how many ways he could divide the Smarties into equal groups. He was limited to 2, 4, 5 and 10.

Teacher: 'You now need to share all the Smarties equally between four people. Can you write that down?'

Peter: *'That's easy. You just split the tens in half.'*

Teacher: 'How many Smarties will each person get?'

Peter: *'Five.'*

Teacher: 'Now write it.'

Peter: *'Is it twenty first?'*

*He looked at his previous example and correctly wrote 20 ÷ 4 = 5, in his book.*

The teacher then wrote 20 ÷ 5 in his book and asked him to write the answer. *He used the Smarties and took five away each time. 'Is the answer five?' he asked. When he was assured that it was, he said, 'It's like adding and multiplying, they're opposites!'*

5. Activity (large group)

Using the multiplication squares produced earlier in this programme and the previous discovery of the group that multiplication was repeated addition, **Peter was able to explore the fact that division was repeated subtraction.** The group was given examples of multiplication and division to help the children to become fluent in the use of the multiplication square.

**Peter's teacher asked him how he felt about mathematics now. His answer was, 'I can do it now.'**

*Assessment of progress (Stage 3)*

a) Accuracy of symbolic recording

This was the most successful element in Peter's programme. He was not only able to record accurately, but was using meaningful symbolic recording to devise his own strategies for solving problems.

For example:

Teacher:    'There were twenty loaves of bread in the shop. Seven were sold. How many loaves were left in the shop?'

Peter:    **'How many loaves were there?'**

Teacher:    'Twenty.'

Peter:    **'How many got sold?'**

Teacher:    'Seven.'

**Peter jotted down the numbers 20 and 7. He then said, 'If I put 10 to one side, I can do it (Figure 24). Then I take the 7 from the 10 (he used a number line for this). Then I put the 10 back. That's 13 ... is it right?'**

Teacher:    'Yes, well done!'

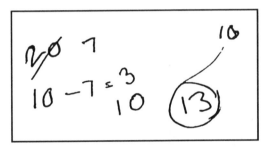

*Figure 24.*

Although he still reversed numbers, he was able to correct many of his own mistakes.

b) Recall of number facts

Assessment in this area was carried out through presenting Peter with a variety of questions both verbal and written, and although his responses were seldom spontaneous, he used the small amount of knowledge he had to help him to solve problems. He could visualise all number facts to six, and use 'double'. He also made good use of a number line and his multiplication square. Some of his strategies were evident on his assessment paper *(Figure 24).*

**Conclusion**

Through his involvement in a successful learning process, Peter had experienced feelings of achievement and satisfaction. Hopefully, this will give him the confidence to continue to form further concepts, see relationships and patterns in numbers which will help him make generalisations and devise strategies in investigational situations.

This will all be put to the test during the following school term, when his teacher hopes that he will be able to make a valuable contribution to a major problem solving activity planned for the whole school. Year 6 pupils are putting on a play. The organisation of the event is to be a whole school effort. Selected pupils from each class have met with the headteacher and drawn up a plan and tasks have been allocated to each year group. Peter's class will be responsible for ordering, making and serving refreshments. His teacher is confident that he will be able to make a valuable contribution.

Mathematics is only useful to the extent to which it can be applied to real life situations. This really will be the test.

## Chapter 5 – Implications for Classroom Teachers

This concluding chapter intends to demonstrate that individualised programmes of study for pupils with SpLD in mathematics need not involve an increase in the workload of the classroom teacher if seen as an integral part of whole school planning.

### Implications for planning

When planning for maximum access to the full breadth and balance of the school curriculum for all pupils, schools generally apply a three-staged model, long term, medium term and short term. Planning for 'individualised programmes' should be evident at all three stages thus preventing 'planning overload' at classroom level.

*Long-term planning*   is concerned with planning the management of the whole school curriculum, including the allocation of teaching time to each individual subject.

What to do

Here classroom teachers and SENCOs could request that extra time be allocated for pupils with SpLD to finish their work in mathematics and that this be built into the whole school plan.

*Medium-term planning*   is concerned with planning the curriculum for individual subjects, with termly or half-termly objectives, including guidance on resources and teaching strategies, and is usually the responsibility of the mathematics co-ordinator/head of department.

What to do

At the consultative stage classroom teachers could suggest that teaching strategies and teaching resources should be enriched to include a multisensory approach to the teaching and learning of mathematics.

*Short-term planning*   is concerned with the daily or weekly planning for classroom delivery of individual subjects.

What to do

In mathematics, classroom teachers should plan for differentiation through enrichment of both teaching and resources, and should include planning for regrouping where necessary.

### Implications for Individual Education Plans

It is unnecessary for teachers to produce 'special' forms for recording IEPs for individualised programmes. If current forms comply with the requirements of the *Code of Practice* they should be appropriate. *It is not the record form that makes a good IEP but the appropriateness of the education plan itself.*

## Implications for assessment

Teachers should use what is already available in terms of National Curriculum Teacher Assessment, extending their observations to include:

- assessment of the pupil's abilities and strategies;

- evaluation of the pupil's response to specific assessment procedures to determine his or her learning style;

- assessment of links with language/reading factors;

- observation of use of apparatus and mathematics instruments;

- parent interviews.

## Implications for classroom practice

By including the following items in general classroom practice, access to the mathematics curriculum for the pupil SpLD could be maximised:

- including something to see, something to listen to and something to do at each new stage in mathematical development;

- capitalising on classroom opportunities for group activities and discussion;

- allowing plenty of time for discussion;

- rehearsing, as appropriate, earlier stages prior to the introduction of new challenges;

- offering opportunities for the wider extension of abilities rather than repetitive practice;

- using strategies both capitalising on pupil's strengths and resources and remediation in areas of weakness/deficiency;

- having regard for the pupils' attitudes and level of confidence;

- being sensitive to the implications of pupil responses;

- continuing attention to transfer and generalisation, including opportunity for formulating formal maths from reality situations;

- planning for future activities, involving the pupil in decision making.

Above all, optimism and encouragement on the part of the teacher should be present at all stages.

# References and Further Reading

Bental, L M (1976) *Essential Mathematics Tests.* NFER-Nelson: London.

Bental, L M (1986) *Mathematics with Meaning.* Stanley Thornes: Cheltenham.

Brennan, W K (1985) *Curriculum for Special Needs.* Open University Press: Milton Keynes.

British Dyslexia Association (undated) *Specific Learning Difficulties in Mathematics.*

Department of Education and Science (1982) *Mathematics Counts: Report of the Committee of Inquiry into the Teaching of Mathematics in Schools (The Cockcroft Report).* HMSO: London.

Department for Education (1994) *The Code of Practice on the Identification and Assessment of Special Educational Needs.* HMSO: London.

Department for Education (1995) *Mathematics in the National Curriculum.* HMSO: London.

Denvir, B (1986) 'Understanding of number concepts in low attaining 7-9 year olds.' *Educational Studies in Mathematics* 17, pp 143–64.

El-Naggar, O (1995) *Investigations and Problem Solving.* QED: Lichfield.

France, N (1979) *Profile of Mathematical Skills.* NFER-Nelson: London.

Gillham, W E C and Hesse, K A (1976) *Basic Number Screening Test.* Hodder and Stoughton Educational: London.

Hagues and Courtenay, (1994) *Mathematics 7-11 Test Series.* NFER-Nelson: London.

Miles, T R and Miles, E (eds) (1992) *Dyslexia and Mathematics.* Routledge: London.

SCAA (1995) *Planning the Curriculum at Key Stages 1 and 2.* SCAA: London.

Skemp, R (1971) *The Psychology of Learning Mathematics.* Penguin: Harmondsworth.

Snowling, M and Thompson, M (eds) (1991) *Dyslexia, Integrating Theory and Practice.* Whurr Publications: London.